Splash

by:

Jocelyn Busato

Based on a True Story

Thanks to the following people:

To my friends for all of their help
and for encouraging me to write this book.

To the students and teachers at SES,
especially Mrs. McComack and Mrs. Zimmerman
for their encouragement and fundraising
to make this book possible.

To my church family at New Stanton United Methodist
Church for their prayers, support, and fundraising.

To my teammates and coaches on the Mount Pleasant
Aqua Club for always pushing me to do my best.

To Brad Allshouse for riding the Tour de Cure
in my honor each year.

To my doctors and diabetes educators at
Children's Hospital in Pittsburgh
for taking good care of me.

A special thanks
to my parents, brothers, Nana, and Pappy,
for their support, love,
and for helping me with my disease.

And finally,

I thank God for always having a plan
and watching over me.

Prologue

"Swimmers, take your mark." Beep!

A chill ran down my spine as I cut into the freezing water. I looked to my right and left to see if anyone was ahead of me. "Yes!" I said to myself. "I'm in the lead!" My dive had gotten me ahead, for now. After a few dolphin kicks, I surfaced and immediately heard the ear-piercing shrieks from the bleachers. "Go!" and "You can do better than that!" rang clear from the whir of voices screaming out from the stands.

I took my first stroke with a nervous feeling breathing down my neck. My legs worked their magic, leaving a trail of white water spurring from my feet. By now I had made it to the far end of the pool. As I approached the wall, I held my breath, tucked, flipped, and sprang off of the tile-covered wall. "Lap two," I said to myself. My flipturn propelled me further away from the other swimmers, but I could still feel them gaining on me. I swam harder. My arms started to feel weak, and my legs ached. I pushed the hurt away and performed my second flipturn.

On lap three, I wasn't feeling so good. My legs were stiff as bricks and my arms felt as flimsy as a noodle. I saw the swimmer in lane four approaching, so I kicked harder. Something deep in my leg started to sting. "Come on!" I screamed to myself. I couldn't push the feeling away. I was overjoyed when I came to the final lap. My flipturn was terrible, but by now I couldn't care less. With my arms flapping, legs pounding, heart racing, and head spinning, I neared the finish. I drove my arm into the wall and sunk back into the water. "I did it," I said, staring amazed at the scoreboard. "I won the championship race." As I was handed a trophy at the swim banquet, I thought back to late November when a boy told me that swimming wasn't a sport. Yeah, right!

Chapter 1
Swimming

"I just want to congratulate everyone. You all did amazing." Sandy, my swimming instructor gushed after handing out the awards. "You should feel proud of yourself." I couldn't help but blush when she said that, considering she was looking straight at me. I smoothed out my skirt, tucked my hair back, and mouthed, "Thanks, Sandy."

It felt almost odd being one of the only people with four first-place trophies. Alongside my brother Alex, we stole the show. "You both did awesome. I'm so proud of you!" my mother said as she gave us both a hug.

I was somewhat relieved that the season was over, so now I could relax. But, I was going to miss splashing around and having fun with my teammates. I get a rush when I swim that I can't get anywhere else. I don't know what it is about it, but I do know this: I love to swim.

I couldn't wait to open our pool in the summer. In Pennsylvania, you only get about three months to enjoy the sunshine, and then before you know it, it's back to school and cold weather. So, our family tries to get into the water as soon as possible. We try to open our pool in May, but sometimes I wish we opened it in April. I can't wait a whole month to swim!

It was early May when we finally opened our pool. Even though the water was so cold it was numbing, I was still excited to jump in and splash around. It felt so good to swim again. I couldn't wait for next season. I could just see it all unfold. Me, driving my hand into the wall and looking up at a scoreboard and seeing a record time. Yes, I couldn't wait for next season.

✿ ✿ ✿

There was about a week left in school when I heard about a boy in my school who had something called diabetes. Which is strange, because he looked okay to me. He didn't look sick at all! I wonder what diabetes is?

When it was the last day of school, as soon as I got off the bus I ran onto our deck, pulled the pool cover off and dove in the water. The water was freezing, but I didn't care. It just felt like I was free. Absolutely free.

Chapter 2
Summer

My summer was a never-ending whirlwind of fun. Since my brother Alex qualified for track and field Nationals, we got to travel to Kansas, Missouri and North Carolina. We got to go into the St. Louis Arch, hike through the Great Plains, and splash off of the coast of North Carolina. My favorite part probably would have to be swimming in the cool, salty Atlantic. It felt great to be in the water.

But, the only problem with my spectacular vacation is that my family noticed I had lost a lot of weight and that I was constantly drinking water. I didn't take any notice, but my family got worried. After we got home from our long trip, they took me to the doctor. I got some tests run, and they said to wait for results. The week of waiting was awful. I didn't know what was going on and was extremely scared.

Finally the doctor called back. In a serious tone she said, "Joselyn E. Busato must be escorted to Children's Hospital in Pittsburgh immediately." By now I could barely breathe. I thought about all the kids who die every year from cancer and leukemia, and hoped that the doctors would just say, "We wanted to congratulate you on being such a cooperative kid" or "All you need is a checkup." I knew that would never happen, but at least I was thinking positive!

My mom, dad, and I all anxiously climbed into our white van. The drive to Pittsburgh was full of worries, silence, and nervousness. I watched the rain spatter down onto the transparent glass of my backseat window, and tried my hardest to swallow back my tears. "What do you think they want?" I asked quietly. "I don't know, honey," my father replied. I could tell he was worried too.

My heart raced as we stepped through the doors to the hospital. I squeezed my mom's hand tighter, and we walked to one of the desks where a lady in purple told us to wait on the couches until we were called back. I sat on my daddy's lap and watched a shiny blue tang swim by in the coral-filled aquarium. "I hope I can still swim," I thought, "and I hope I'll be okay." I waited anxiously for what seemed like days, and then finally a nurse called out my name. I hesitated. My dad and mom held my hands, and helped me find the courage to step into a cold room with a bed in the center.

Before I knew what was happening, a lady with white gloves stuck a needle in my left arm. "It's an IV," she said, "so we can monitor you more easily." I had no idea what she was talking about, and it didn't help when she left with a tube of blood and a serious look on her face without saying a word.

The doctor who gave me the IV was now rolling me down a hallway into an elevator. My wheelchair was soft and cushy, but the aching worry in my heart made it feel

as hard as a brick. I still didn't know what was wrong with me. All the doctor said was, "Yep, the results came back positive." I thought to myself, "Maybe it's a good thing, because they said "positive".

When I made it to my room, the doctor said I would have to stay there for about four days. I wasn't happy about this, but I didn't have the energy to complain. So, I simply asked one of the doctors, "What do I have?" The lady in white sighed, and looked down at me. " Juvenile Diabetes. Now, are you hungry?" It felt like all the air was knocked out of my chest. Diabetes? How could this happen? All I could squeak out was, "Yes, I am hungry." But inside, I was bawling.

✿ ✿ ✿

The next few days were filled with education, checkups, family visits, and flowers sent with balloons and stuffed animals. I used these to brighten up my gloomy room, along with origami flowers that my brother Alex made me placed in an empty plastic cup, and pictures I drew and hung up on my wall with medical tape. Some days were so boring just being in my room that I made up a "fun" game to play in the morning. I would grab a notebook and pencil and write down observations I saw out of my hospital window.

"Two women with alligator purses are giggling about something. One of them just jumped up and down. Now she's crying. Odd. Now there's a guy on a bicycle with a blue shirt and red tie. He has flowers in his right hand and steering with the left. Uh-oh, he just used his left hand to push up his glasses. He's swerving! Oh, he caught himself. A couple in black clothes just marched across the street into a white house. A man in a blue jumpsuit is walking a Boston Terrier…"

When I finally got out of the hospital, a thought shot into my mind. "Will I be able to swim again?" I started to panic. With a worried tone in my voice, I asked my parents if I would be able to swim. They replied, "I'm sure you can, but you will just have to monitor yourself." If you don't know what that means, then here you go: I have to check my blood sugar whenever I eat, or when I'm doing an activity. Swimming would definitely count as an activity. So, the question is, "Will I be able to swim?" Only time will tell.

Chapter 3
Again

When the season started back up, I was a nervous wreck. The only thing in my mind was, "Will I be able to swim?" I had no idea. I kept thinking about it, and thinking about it, until finally the first day of practice came.

I splashed down into the water and started to paddle. For a second I felt relaxed, but then the nervous feeling shot back into my mind. I took a deep breath, calmed myself down and kept swimming.

Halfway through the practice, the thing I was imagining became a reality. My arms began to slow down, my vision got blurry, and I started to sink. I pulled my weak body out of the water and dizzily scurried to my swim bag, where I kept a stash of candy. "Low blood sugar?" my dad asked, handing me a lollipop. All I could do was nod my head.

I felt like I was going to cry. The only thing in my mind was that this was going to happen every practice, and furthermore I wouldn't be able to swim again.

The same routine went on for a month, and with each piece of candy my heart grew heavier. Championships were drawing nearer, and I got extremely

worried. I had had a good season so far, but at each meet I had to treat my low blood sugar. I became very worried that during one of my events, or while I'm racing, I'll get low!

Meanwhile, at my house, things were difficult. Before every meal I had to use a needle to prick my finger, and test a sample of my blood. Along with that, I had to give myself injections, plan my meal out, and had to lug around a purse full of candy to all of my classes in school. All of the other students would ask me why I had to have snacks in the middle of class, and why I went to the nurse before lunch. The chance of me doing championships, or even swimming anymore, seemed slim. I didn't know what to do!

When I went to church one day, a few weeks before championships, our bible school lesson was about how God has a plan for all of us. The bible verse that went along with the lesson was Jeremiah 29:11. That verse seemed very familiar. I flipped through the pages and came to rest on the verse that changed my outlook. It was:

"For I know the plans I have for you," says the Lord, "plans to prosper you, and not harm you. Plans to give you a hope, and a future." Jeremiah 29:11

I sat there amazed. That's when it hit me: God gave me diabetes for a reason. He wants me to swim, and I can make it. I just know I can.

At every practice afterwards, I felt stronger. Even with constantly treating low blood sugars, my spirits were sky-high. "I'm gonna do it. I'm going to do championships!

Chapter 4
Championships

My family set up camp for championships in a noisy, crammed gymnasium. A man with scruffy eyebrows was calling event numbers and telling everyone what to do. I was events 4, 19, 29, 39, and 68. As each race grew closer, my heart started to pound harder. Finally, my events were called. A shiver ran down my back. I stepped up to the block, and with my head spinning, dove in.

I gave my relays my all. My "100 IM" left me breathless. Two laps of butterfly made me feel like a noodle, and the "100 freestyle" made me sore beyond compare. When I finished my final race, it finally occurred to me that I had done it! I had made it through the long meet without a single low blood sugar. I was so happy I cried.

I told my family my feelings about Championships, and how God gave me strength. My mom started to tear up, and my dad wouldn't stop grinning. We all collapsed into a hug, and I began to think about the awards banquet. I wonder what I got?

✿ ✿ ✿

"Thank you for coming," Sandy said, "I'm very proud of you all." My mom squeezed my hand tight, and one by one my awards were given to me. One first, one second, one third, one fourth. It wasn't as good as the four first place trophies I received last year, but I was happy and thankful for what I got. God gave me strength, and through faith, I succeeded.

Epilogue

Today, I continue to swim competitively and live with Type 1 Diabetes. I have participated in fundraiser walks and have been given contributions from my church and school in the hope that one day we will find a cure and that my book will give others hope.

I continue to be a lover of and firm believer in God, and have found strength through Jesus Christ.

Made in the USA
Middletown, DE
13 June 2015